Bannockburn School Dist. 106
2165 Telegraph Road
Bannockburn, Illinois 60015

DATE ~~DUE~~

Protein

George Ivanoff

Bannockburn School Dist. 106
2165 Telegraph Road
Bannockburn, Illinois 60015

Smart Apple Media
P.O. Box 3263
Mankato, MN, 56002

First published in 2011 by
MACMILLAN EDUCATION AUSTRALIA PTY LTD
15–19 Claremont St, South Yarra, Australia 3141

Visit our web site at www.macmillan.com.au or go directly to www.macmillanlibrary.com.au

Associated companies and representatives throughout the world.

Copyright Text © George Ivanoff 2011

Library of Congress Cataloging-in-Publication Data has been applied for.

Publisher: Carmel Heron
Commissioning Editor: Niki Horin
Managing Editor: Vanessa Lanaway
Editor: Emma Short
Proofreader: Georgina Garner
Designer: Kerri Wilson
Page layout: Cath Pirret Design
Photo researcher: Sarah Johnson (management: Debbie Gallagher)
Illustrator: Leigh Hedstrom, Flee Illustration
Production Controller: Vanessa Johnson

Manufactured in China by Macmillan Production (Asia) Ltd.
Kwun Tong, Kowloon, Hong Kong
Supplier Code: CP December 2010

Acknowledgments
The author and the publisher are grateful to the following for permission to reproduce copyright material:

Front cover photograph: Boy eating boiled egg, Getty Images/Stockbyte

Photographs courtesy of: Dreamstime/Adehughes, 21, /Alexkalina, 9 (eggs), /Cybernesco, 7 (middle), /Fibobjects, 24 (milk), / Icefront, 7 (bottom left), /Marinadi, 19, /Niderlander, 9 (fish), 24 (fish), /Rmarmion, 14, /Alexander Silaev, 7 (top), /Andrey Starostin, 24 (pasta), /Ukrphoto, 6 (bottom), /Valentyn75, 7 (bottom right), /Ynse, 10; Getty Images/Bob Thomas Sports Photography, 18; iStockphoto/Marina Appel, 26, /Yenwen Lu, 20; Photolibrary/Creatas, 9 (soymilk), /Food Collection, 11, /Till Jacket, 8, /Kablonk!, 4, /Alex Mares-Manton, 22, /Paul Paul, 30, /Saturn Stills/SPL, 23; Pixmac/a4stockphotos, 3, 6 (top); Shutterstock/ilker canikligil, 27 (museli), /geniuscook_com, 24 (cheese), /Givaga, 27 (pasta), /Imageman, 29 (lentils), /iofoto, 5, /majaan, 27 (bread), /MarFot, 24 (cereal), /Monkey Business Images, 13, 16-17, /Morgan Lane Photography, 6 (middle), /nito, 27 (peanuts), /Galayko Sergey, 29 (chickpeas, red beans), /szefei, 27 (rice), /Vasilius, 29 (peas), /Viktor1, 9 (chicken), /Peter zijlstra, 24 (meat).

Contents

When a word is printed in **bold**, you can look up its meaning in the Glossary on page 31.

What's in My Food?

Your food is made up of **nutrients**. Nutrients help your body work, grow, and stay alive.

Nutrients give you **energy** so you can be active.

Different types of food contain different types of nutrients. A **balanced diet** includes food with the right amount of nutrients for your body.

A balanced diet helps keep your body healthy.

What Nutrients Are in My Food?

There are many different types of nutrients in your food. They include proteins, carbohydrates, fats, fiber, minerals, and vitamins.

Protein in meat, poultry, eggs, and fish helps your body grow and heal.

Carbohydrates in bread and pasta give your body energy.

Fats in fish and olive oil give your body energy and help it stay healthy.

Fiber in bread and vegetables helps your body **digest** food.

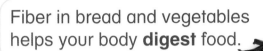

Vitamins in fruit and vegetables help your body work well.

Minerals in milk and meat help your body grow and stay healthy.

Protein

Protein is a nutrient that is in many foods. It helps your body grow and heal. Adults need to eat more protein than children to stay healthy.

Most people need about 0.0128 ounces of protein per pound (0.8 g per kg) of their weight.

Age: 8
Weight: 55 pounds
(25 kg)

This person needs to eat around 0.7 ounces (20 g) of protein every day.

Different types of food have different amounts of protein.

These foods each have 0.7 ounces (20 g) of protein:

3 large eggs

2.8 ounces (80 g) of fish

3 cups of soy milk

2.8 ounces (80 g) of chicken

What Is Protein?

Protein is made up of small parts called **molecules**. You need a microscope to see them.

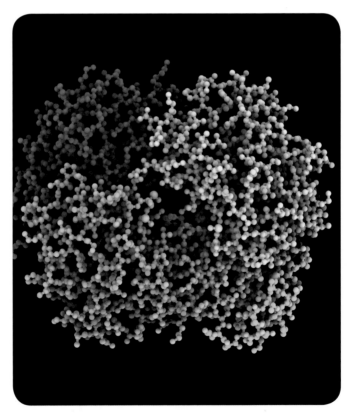

Amino acids join together to form protein.

Protein is a **macronutrient**. Your body needs a lot of macronutrients to stay healthy. Fats and carbohydrates are also macronutrients.

Protein, as well as fats and carbohydrates, can be found in spaghetti and meatballs.

protein ————

fats ————

carbohydrates ————

How Does My Body Get Protein?

Your body **absorbs** protein when you digest food. When food breaks down in your stomach, the protein breaks down into amino acids. The amino acids enter the blood.

food

blood

stomach

Your blood carries amino acids all around your body.

Your body uses amino acids in three ways.

1. Amino acids make new **tissues** that help your body grow.

2. Amino acids give your body **energy**.

3. Amino acids make **hormones** that carry messages to different parts of your body.

What Does Protein Do?

Protein helps your blood carry oxygen to different parts of your body. It gives you energy and helps your body grow. It also helps your body stay healthy.

Protein helps your skin and hair stay healthy.

Protein Carries Oxygen

Protein makes **hemoglobin** (*hee-mah-gloh-bin*) in your blood. Hemoglobin carries oxygen from your lungs to the rest of your body.

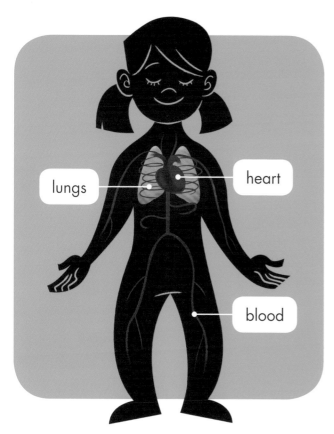

lungs

heart

blood

Protein helps your blood carry oxygen from your lungs around your body.

Protein Powers My Body

Some of the amino acids in protein turn into energy. This energy powers your body, helping you stay active.

Your body needs protein power to stay active all day.

Protein Powers My Brain

The amino acids in protein help keep your brain alert. This helps you to be calm and ready to learn.

Protein helps you think and learn when you do your homework.

Protein Makes Me Strong

Protein helps build your **muscles** and make them strong. It also keeps your heart and lungs strong.

Athletes need a lot of protein because they use their muscles more than most people.

Protein Helps Me Grow

Your body uses protein to make new **cells**. Your body needs cells so that it can grow.

Your body needs protein to help you grow from a baby into an adult.

Protein Helps Me Stay Healthy

Protein helps your body work well. It helps your body heal by fixing damaged cells.

Protein helps to fix cuts and scrapes, and grows cells to make new skin.

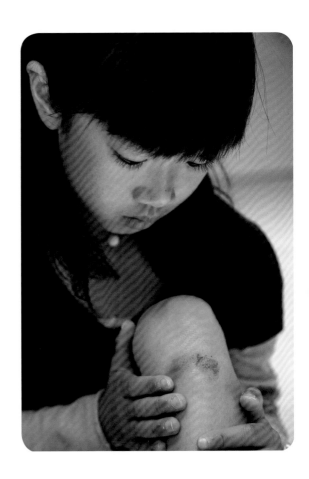

Protein helps protect your body from **infection**. It helps fight **germs** and stops you from getting sick.

When you are sick, protein helps you get better.

Protein Helps Make Hormones

The amino acids in protein help make hormones. Hormones send messages to different parts of your body.

Some hormones tell your body to grow.

The amino acids in protein help make a hormone called insulin. Insulin tells your body how to break down and use sugar.

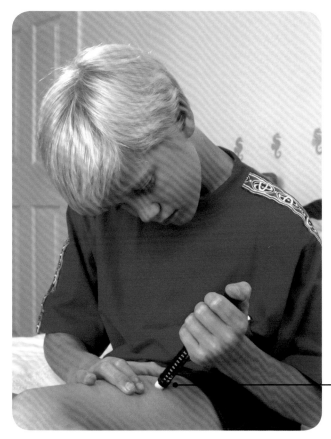

Some people's bodies do not make enough insulin. They need to inject insulin into their bodies using an insulin pen or syringe.

— insulin pen

Which Foods Contain Protein?

Many foods contain protein. Different foods have different types of protein, and your body uses them in different ways. You need to eat foods with protein every day.

All of these foods contain protein.

cereal

red meat

milk

cheese

pasta

Foods with protein are part of a balanced diet. Other foods also have nutrients that your body needs, such as vitamins and minerals. You need to eat these foods too.

A balanced diet includes many different kinds of foods, as well as water.

dairy foods

nuts, seeds, and grains

bread, cereal, rice, pasta, and noodles

water

fruit, vegetables, and legumes

meat, poultry, fish, and eggs

Protein Is in Dairy Foods

Dairy foods are made from milk. Dairy foods, such as yogurt and cheese, contain protein.

Dairy foods also contain a mineral called calcium, which keeps your bones and teeth healthy.

Protein Is in Nuts, Seeds, and Grains

Nuts and seeds have protein. Grains, such as wheat, rice, and oats, also have protein. These grains contain carbohydrates and fiber, too.

Nuts, seeds, and grains are used to make bread, breakfast cereals, and pasta.

nuts

seeds and grains

used to make

bread

breakfast cereal

pasta

Protein Is in Meat, Poultry, Fish, and Eggs

Meat, such as lamb, beef, and pork, has a lot of protein. Fish, eggs, and poultry, such as chicken and turkey, have protein too.

Eating a balance of these foods will help give your body the protein it needs.

Protein Is in Legumes

Some vegetables, called legumes, have protein. They include peas, beans, and lentils. Soy milk and tofu are made from legumes called soybeans, which also have protein. Some people drink soy milk, instead of cow's milk, to get protein.

Peas, chickpeas, beans, and lentils are all kinds of legumes.

peas

chickpeas

beans

lentils

What Happens if I Don't Eat Protein?

If you don't eat protein, your body can't make new cells or fix damaged ones. You won't grow, and you might get sick. Your muscles will start to break down.

If you don't eat protein, your body will not grow or stay healthy.

Hair and fingernails will not grow.

Muscles will become weak.

Damaged cells will not heal.

Glossary

absorbs	takes in
balanced diet	a healthy selection of food that you eat
cells	the smallest living parts of a living thing
digest	to break down food in the body
energy	the ability to be active
germs	tiny living things that make you sick
hemoglobin	protein molecules that carry oxygen
hormones	chemicals in the body
infection	the spread of germs or a disease
macronutrient	a nutrient that the body needs a lot of
molecules	very small parts in food
muscles	parts of the body that help you move
nutrients	the healthy parts of food that people need to live
oxygen	a gas in the air that living things need to breathe
tissues	substances in your body that help you grow

Index